ROBERT FRANK / THE LINES OF MY HAND

ROBERT FRANK
THE LINES OF MY HAND

PANTHEON BOOKS, NEW YORK

Copyright © 1989 by Robert Frank

All rights reserved under International and Pan-American Copyright Conventions.
Published in the United States by Pantheon Books, a division of Random House, Inc., New York,
and simultaneously in Canada by Random House of Canada Limited, Toronto.

Originally published in different form in Japan as a limited artist's edition by Kazuhiko Motomura in 1972, copyright © 1972 by Robert Frank.
This completely revised version edited by Robert Frank and Walter Keller.
Cover by June Leaf. Design by Werner Zryd. Duotones and color separations by Litho AG, Aarau/Switzerland. Printed by Steidl, Göttingen, Germany.
Simultaneously published in Europe by Walter Keller, Parkett/Der Alltag Publishers Ltd., Zurich-Frankfurt-New York,
and in the United Kingdom by Martin Secker & Warburg Limited, London.

Library of Congress Cataloging-in-Publication Data

Frank, Robert
  The lines of my hand
  1. Photography, Artistic. 2. Photography,
  Documentary. I. Title.
TR654.F7 1989   779'.092   89-42660

ISBN 0-394-55255-5

First American Edition

I HAVE COME HOME AND I'M LOOKING THROUGH THE WINDOW.
Outside it's snowing, no waves at all. The beach is white, the fence posts are grey. I am looking back into a world now gone forever. Thinking of a time that will never return. A book of photographs is looking at me. Twenty-five years of looking for the right road. Post cards from everywhere. If there are any answers I have lost them.

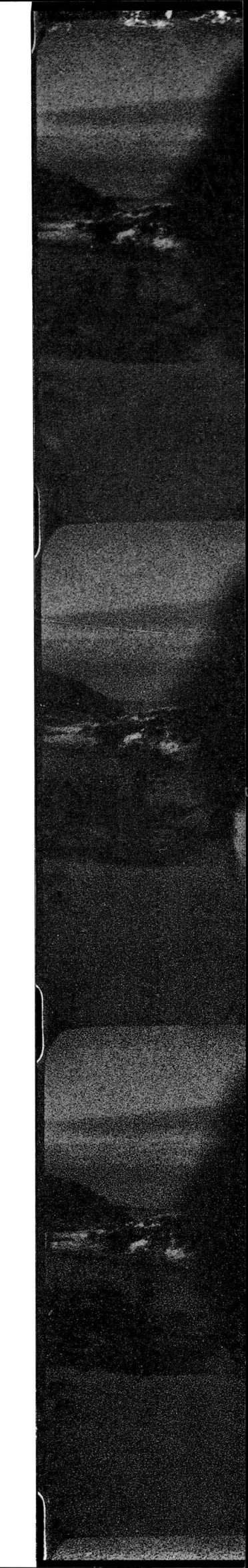

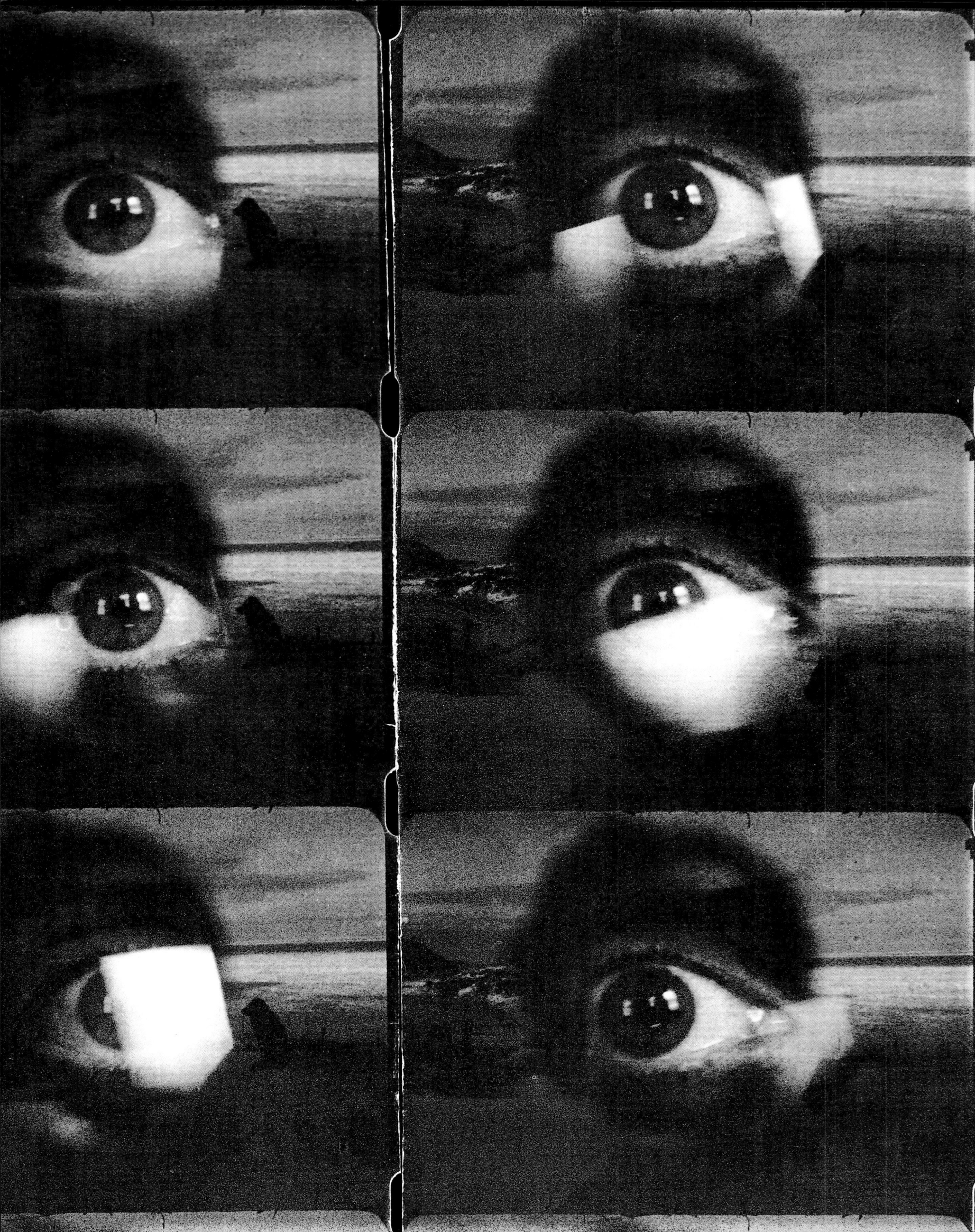

HERE TOGETHER FOR THE FIRST AND ONLY TIME SOME OF MY FRIENDS now gone forever Teddy Gross and his friend Bob Thompson and to Rachel Armour, to Jack Kerouac to Gaby's father to Ben Schultz and to Gotthard Schuh to Shane O'Neill and to Paddy from 23rd Street to Freddy Nield and to Stanley Sulzer to San-Yu to Jan Müller and to Saint George Brian so that we remember… a little bit longer

(1972)

Above all for Pablo and Andrea

who are trying to find a better way to live

1944–1946 PHOTOGRAPHS IN SWITZERLAND. I want to get away, further ... to America

March 1947 – I arrive at New York Harbour. A new life begins. I thought: I AM LUCKY

NEW YORK CITY March 14th 1947 – February 1951

11TH STREET AND BROADWAY

CENTRAL PARK SOUTH

ASTOR PLACE

WHITE TOWER, 14TH STREET

MACY PARADE

53 EAST 11TH STREET, BENNY

WALL STREET

34TH STREET

WALL STREET

FOR ALEXY BRODOVITCH

CROSBY STREET

MARY AND PABLO

PARIS 1949–1951

LONGCHAMP

CHAMPS ELYSÉES, NOVEMBER 11TH

AVENUE DU MAINE

14ÈME, FÊTE FORAINE

JANUARY 1ST 1949

PLACE DE L'ETOILE

BARCELONA

BARCELONA

VALENCIA

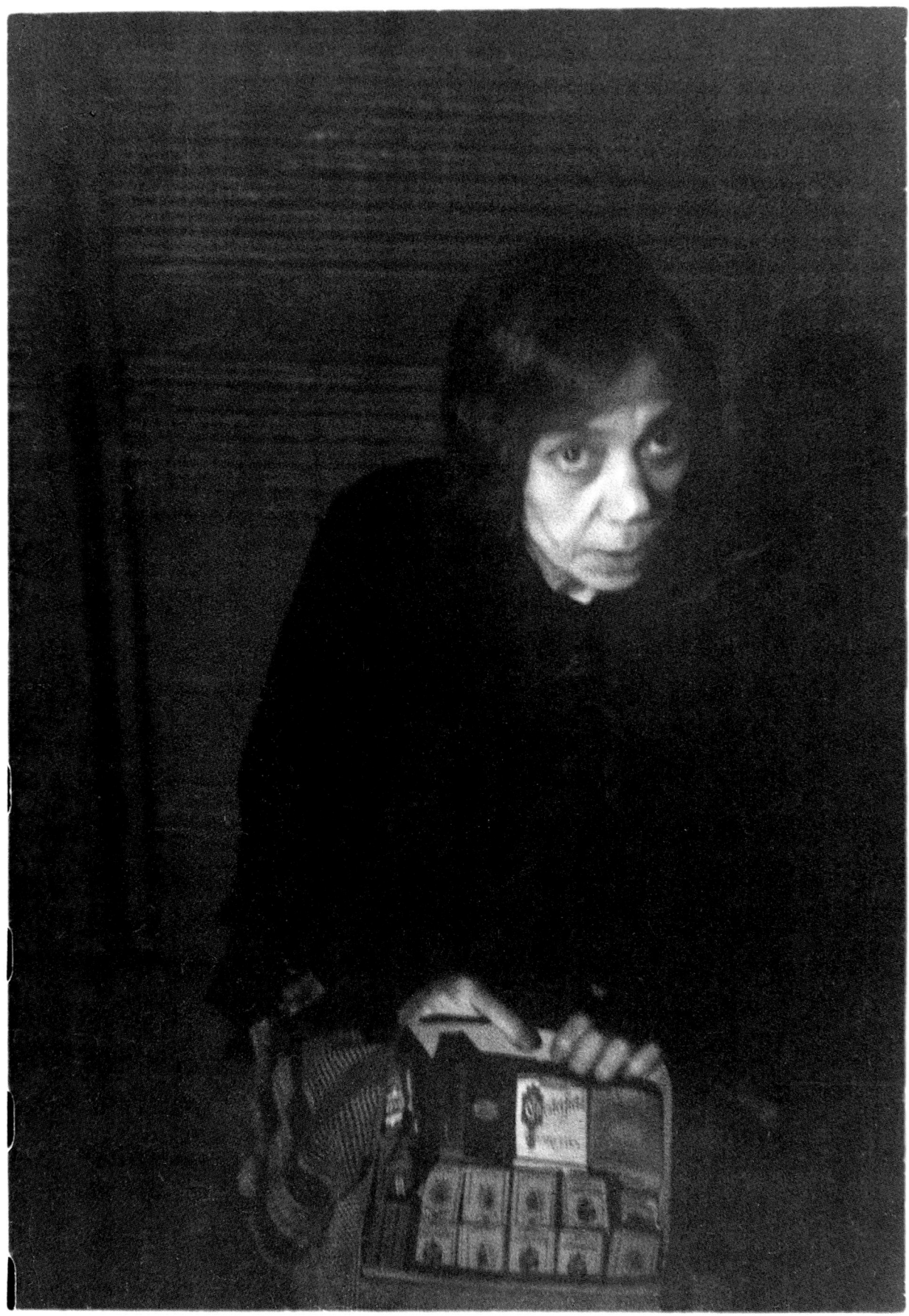

BARCELONA

VALENCIA

ANDRAITX, MALLORCA

LONDON and WALES 1952–1953

CAERAU, WALES

WALES

NEAR VICTORIA STATION, LONDON

CITY OF LONDON

HAMPSTEAD

BELSIZE CRESCENT

PARKING LOT

APPROACHING NEW YORK HARBOUR

I met JACK KEROUAC on a hot summer night – a party in New York City. We sat down on the side walk, I showed Jack the photographs for «The Americans». He said: «Sure I can write something about these pictures...»

«I told you to wait in the car» SAY PEOPLE IN AMERICA SO ROBERT SNEAKS AROUND AND PHOTOGRAPHS LITTLE KIDS WAITING IN THE CAR, WHETHER THREE LITTLE BOYS IN A MOTORAMA LIMOUSINE, OMPIOUS & OPIFUL, OR POOR LITTLE KIDS CAN'T KEEP THEIR EYES OPEN ON ROUTE 90 TEXAS AT 4 A.M. AS DAD GOES TO THE BUSHES AND STRETCHES – THE GASOLINE MONSTERS STAND IN THE NEW MEXICO FLATS UNDER BIG SIGN SAYS SAVE – THE SWEET LITTLE WHITE BABY IN THE BLACK NURSE'S ARMS BOTH OF THEM BEMUSED IN HEAVEN, A PICTURE THAT SHOULD HAVE BEEN BLOWN UP AND HUNG IN THE STREET OF LITTLE ROCK SHOWING LOVE UNDER THE SKY AND IN THE WOMB OF OUR UNIVERSE THE MOTHER – AND THE LONELIEST PICTURE EVER MADE, THE URINALS THAT WOMEN NEVER SEE, THE SHOESHINE GOING ON IN SAD ETERNITY –

UNITED STATES 1955–1956

SOUTH CAROLINA, ORAL ROBERTS ON TV

KIDS: What are you doing here? Are you from New York? – ME: I'm just taking pictures. – KIDS: Why? – ME: For myself – just to see… – KIDS: He must be a communist. He looks like one. Why don't you go to the other side of town and watch the niggers play?

IN FRONT OF HIGH SCHOOL, PORT GIBSON, MISSISSIPPI, 1955

AND I SAY: That little lonely elevator girl looking up sighing in an elevator full of blurred demons, what's her name and address?   JACK KEROUAC

MIAMI

CHICAGO LOOP

TEXACO CAFE, TEXAS

RIVER ROUGE PLANT, DETROIT

TV STUDIO, HOLLYWOOD

CENTRAL CASTING, HOLLYWOOD

DETROIT MOVIE HOUSE

DETROIT GREYHOUND STATION

HOOVER DAM, NEVADA

LOS ANGELES

JULY 4TH 1958, CONEY ISLAND

WASHINGTON, D.C.

HIGHWAY 40, DELAWARE

PENNSYLVANIA AVENUE, WASHINGTON, D.C.

THESE PHOTOGRAPHS REPRESENT MY LAST PROJECT IN PHOTOGRAPHY. When I selected the pictures and put them together I knew and I felt that I had come to the end of a chapter. And in it was the beginning of something new...

BUS PHOTOGRAPHS, NEW YORK CITY, 1958

TO MAKE FILMS...

IN MAKING FILMS I CONTINUE TO LOOK AROUND ME, but I am no longer the solitary observer turning away after the click of the shutter. Instead I'm trying to recapture what I saw, what I heard and what I feel. What I know! There is no decisive moment, it's got to be created. I've got to do everything to make it happen in front of the lens:

SEARCHING__   EXPLAINING__   DIGGING__

                                                               WATCHING__   JUDGING__   ERASING__

                     PRETENDING__   DISTORTING__   LYING__   JUDGING__   RECORDING__

                           TRYING__   TRYING__   TRYING__

     RUNNING__   TELLING A TRUTH__   RUNNING__   CRAWLING__

                                                                  WORKING TOWARDS THE TRUTH__

                                                                       UNTIL IT IS DONE

Pull my daisy, tip my cup, all my doors are open, all my thoughts for coconuts, all my prayers awaken, start my garden, gait my shades, now my life is spoken.

PULL MY DAISY – NARRATED BY JACK KEROUAC. ROBERT FRANK & ALFRED LESLIE, 1959

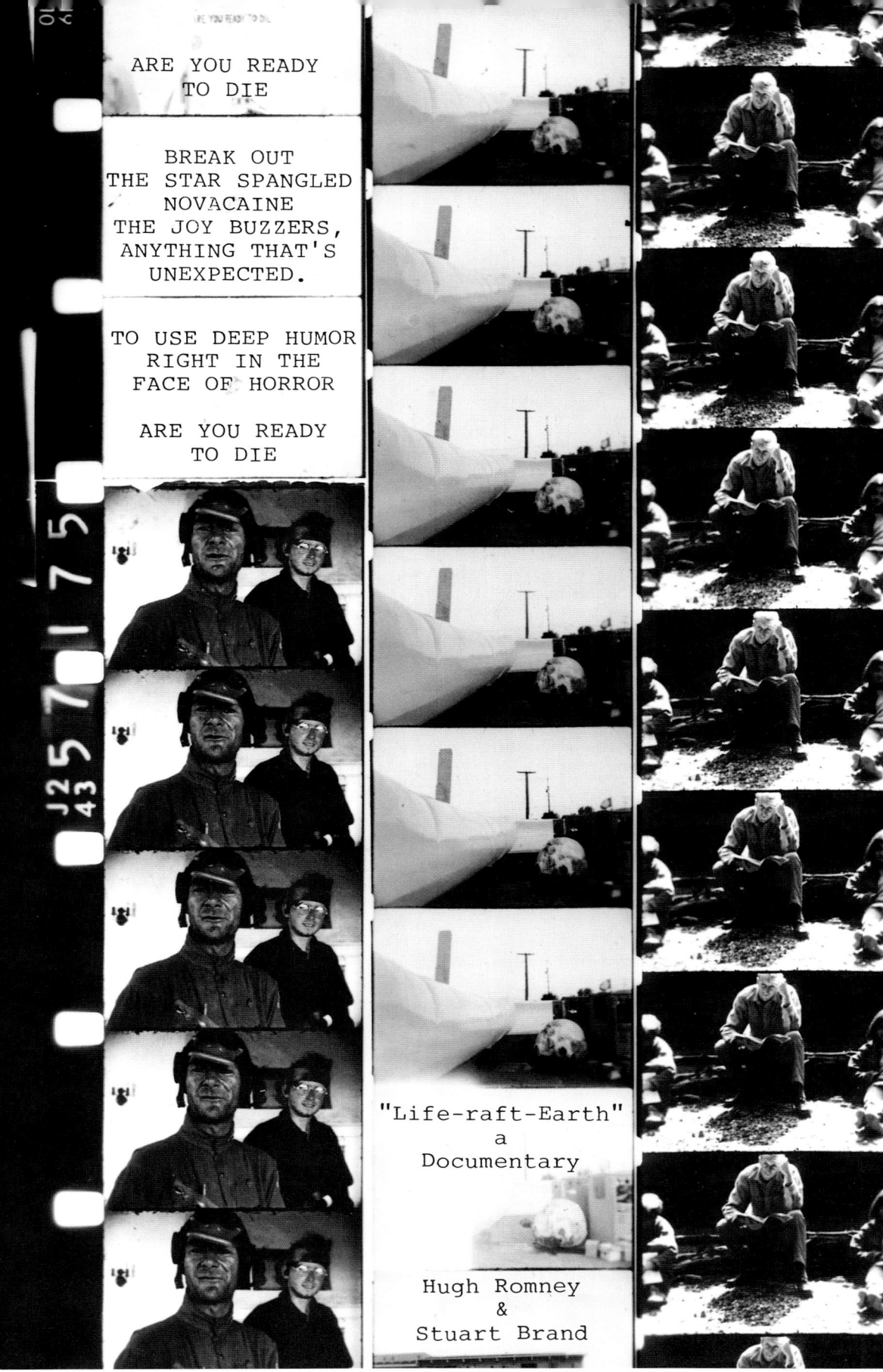

THIS IS THE FIRST BATTLE of a war against death. And death is starvation and ignorance. And ignorance and starvation are death, they go together and there is still a little bit of time where people could do something about it – if they became aware of what it is that they are doing here on this planet.

LIFE – RAFT – EARTH, OCTOBER 1970

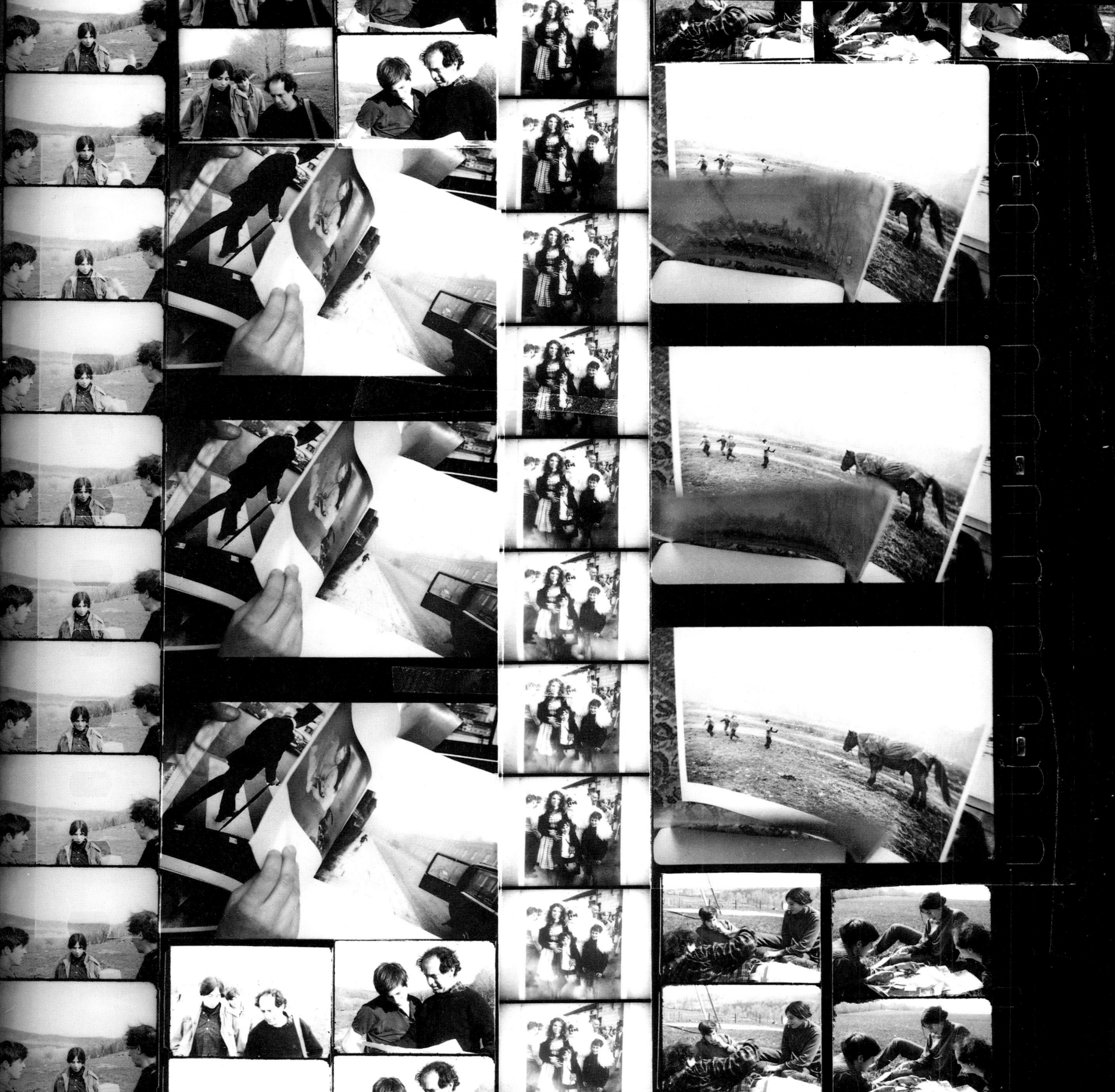

PABLO and ANDREA go to school in Vermont. I went there to confront them and myself with camera and microphone and photos of the past.
A tense and painful experience for all three of us.

CONVERSATIONS IN VERMONT, 1969

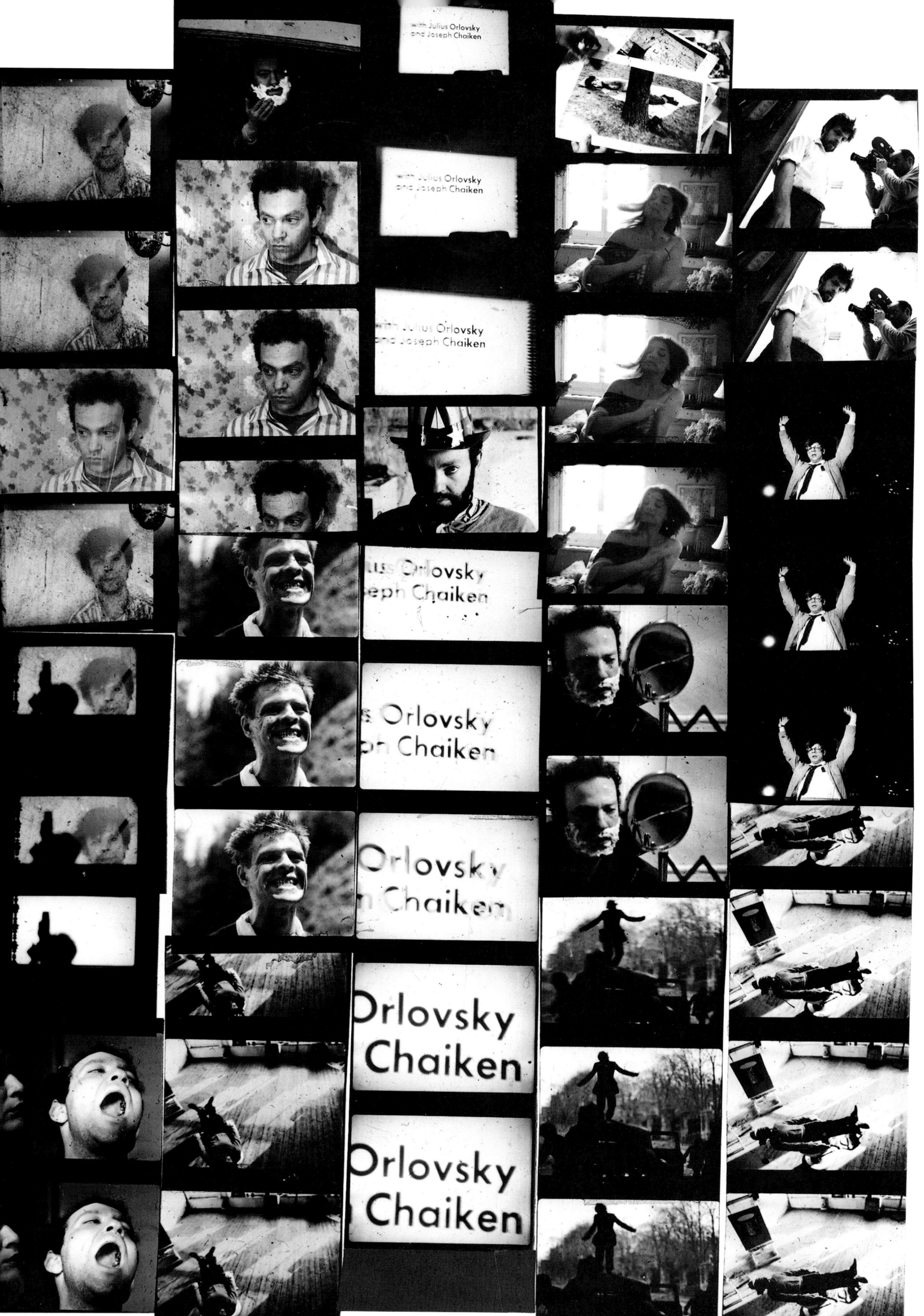

A FILM ABOUT A SILENT MAN AND AN ACTOR WHO BECAME SILENT.

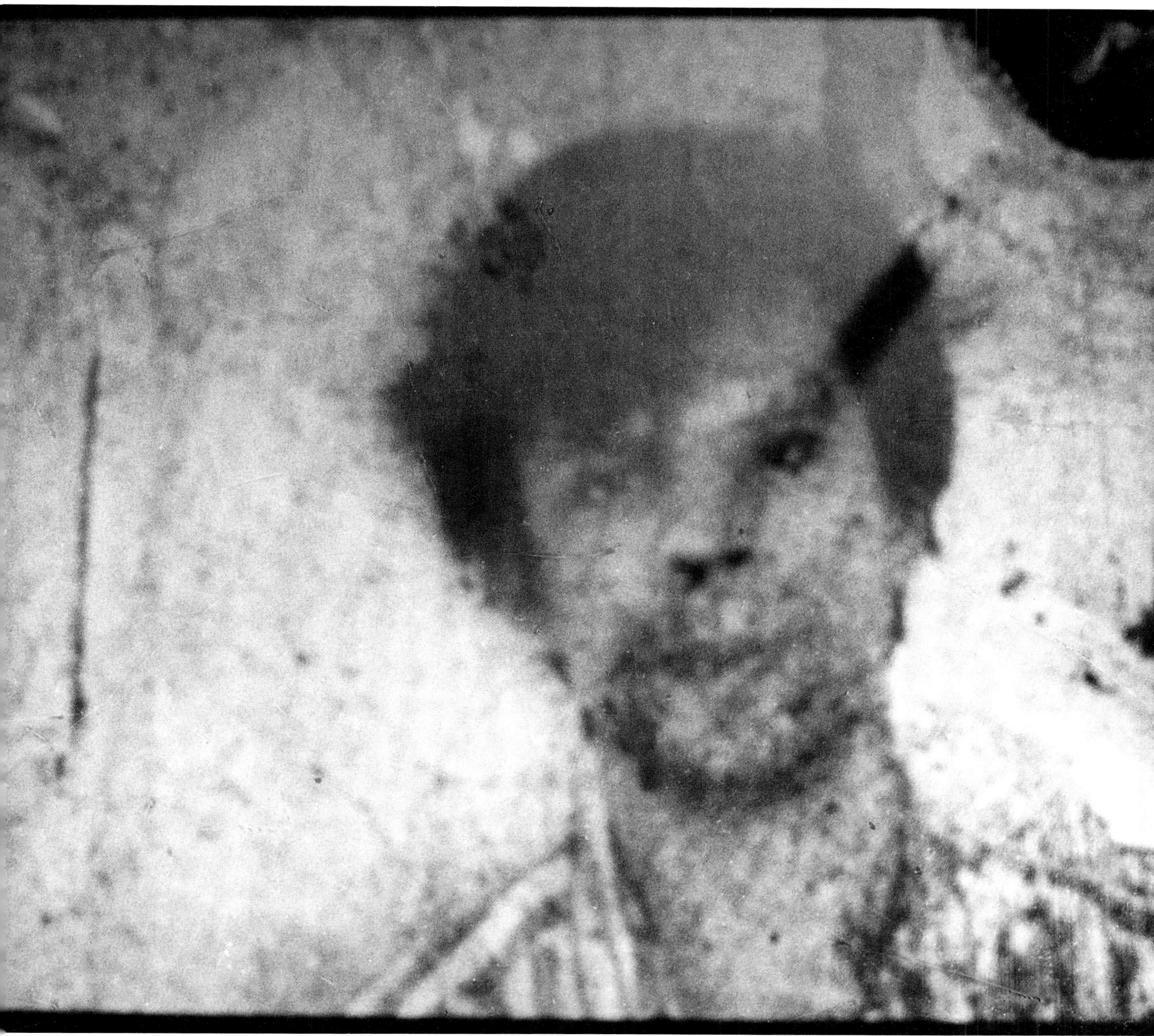

THE ACTOR – JOSEPH CHAIKEN: What's next? My speech is all used up. I have nothing else to say. Nothing else to read from. I don't know what to play. Who should I be? Who should I play?

THE SILENT MAN – JULIUS ORLOVSKY: I can't confide in my friends. It makes you sick, talking, talking makes me sick. It's sad boy – it's sad. I silently became a friend of myself. I'm silently making up with myself, trying to be friendly with myself, smoothing myself up. Dig me, sometimes it's too late to meet your friends.

ME AND MY BROTHER, 1965–1968

BEGINS AS A DOCUMENTARY – turns into fiction and fusion.

INVENTOR ROBERT GOLKA   Wendover Nevada 1979

ENERGY AND HOW TO GET IT. ROBERT FRANK, RUDY WURLITZER, GARY HILL, 1981

IT'S TRUE. I don't believe in words, but you can always add something of your own to make it honest.

SPONTANEOUS MUSIC – REHEARSED ACTING. ABOUT ME – A MUSICAL, NEW YORK CITY, 1971

ROLLING STONES AMERICAN TOUR, 1972   COCKSUCKER BLUES, ROBERT FRANK, DANIEL SEYMOUR

JULIUS: «The whole deal went up in flames. The next morning it was really cold. I guess it's always cold when you're leaving.»

CANDY MOUNTAIN, ROBERT FRANK & RUDY WURLITZER, 1987

YES IT'S LATER NOW... The ice is breaking up, the water will be warm and blue. The boats will be out there. The hills will look green again. Will we go back to New York? Just stay and watch the weather and television? June is looking through the microscope. I will do SOMETHING. Isn't it wonderful just to be alive.

IN NOVA SCOTIA Canada

Mabou 1977 Robert Frank

YOU SHOULDN'T BE POINTING THE CAMERA. My innermost thoughts is my secret. I wish you wouldn't do that. That's invading my privacy, you understand? Otherwise I'm speaking externally when I should be thinking internally and you shouldn't do that.   BILLY

MARTY making magic books, playing music in a crazy New York street. Blockbuster. Fireworks. Hold on. Life dances on…   MARTY

LIFE DANCES ON, 1980

WHAT'S IN YOUR HAND, PABLO? The moon and the stars – the star of David and a flying saucer. What is it again? The earth and the ice in the desert. JOB 38:22 «Have you visited the Storehouse of Snow, seen the Arsenal where Hail is stored.» PABLO AND SANDY

WE MEET IN NEW YORK. He is young – crazy about images. We become friends. Daniel Seymour travels fast. We work together – it ended with Cocksucker Blues. Fate. And Danny will never return from his last trip. GOOD BYE – CUT

FEBRUARY 7TH 1979. HAPPY BIRTHDAY PABLO. What a hard life we have together. I can't take it. Too much for me. It was March, it rained like hell, I got you a one-way ticket to Winslow, Arizona. You said: I want to look at the Meteor – falling from the Sky. Good luck I said – and drove away…

NEW YEARS DAY 1981

BE HAPPY

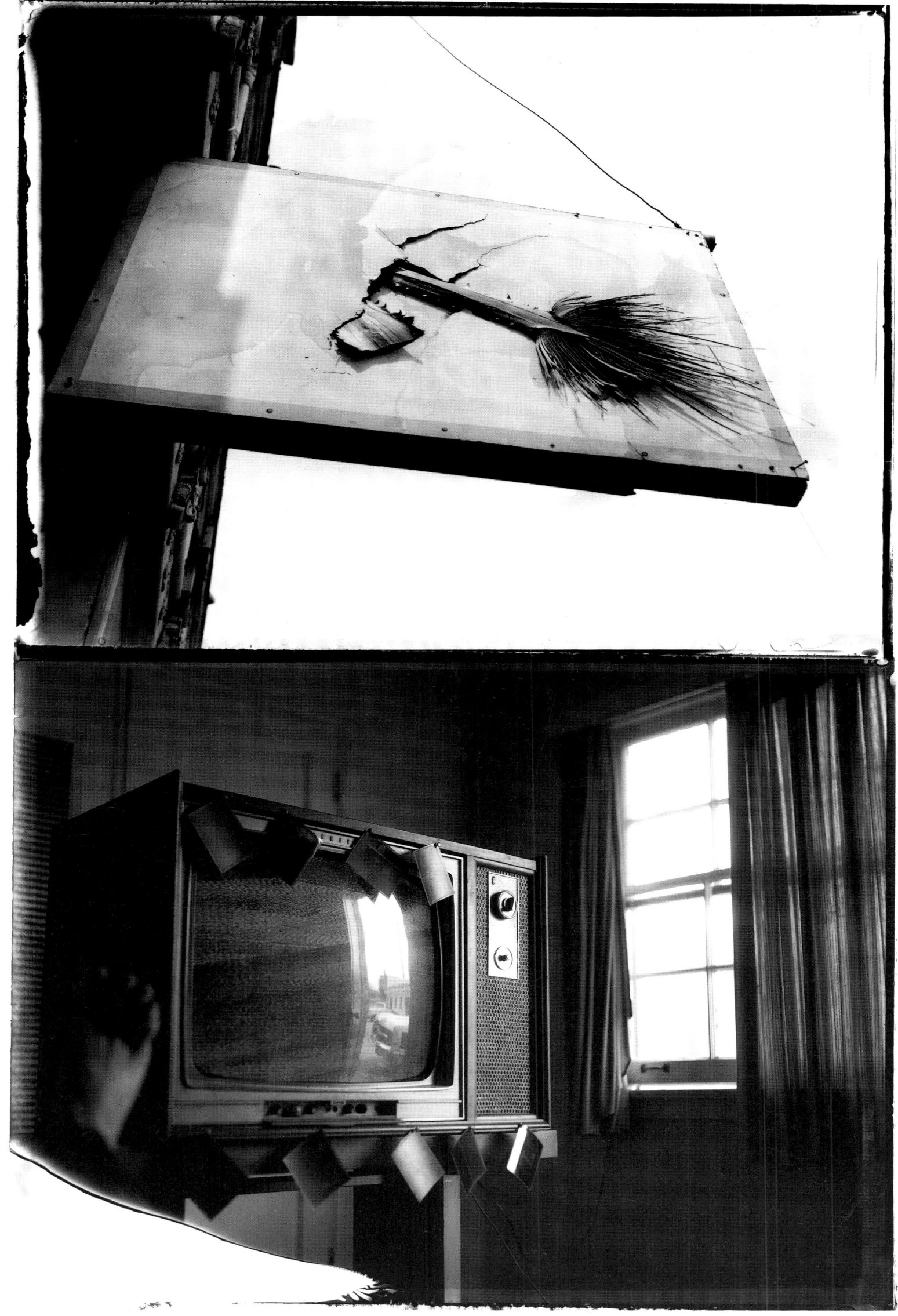

MOVING-OUT

LONG GONE SHADOW OF MARRIAGE ON THIRD AVE LOFT

FORGOTTEN POSESSIONS IN JOHN TURNERS FINAL ROOM / LAST LOOK AT MY PARENTS WOHNZIMMER IN ZURICH

New York City 1979 Robert Frank

the East America

VIDEO: HOME IMPROVEMENTS, November 1983–February 1984

DADDY is looking for the truth...

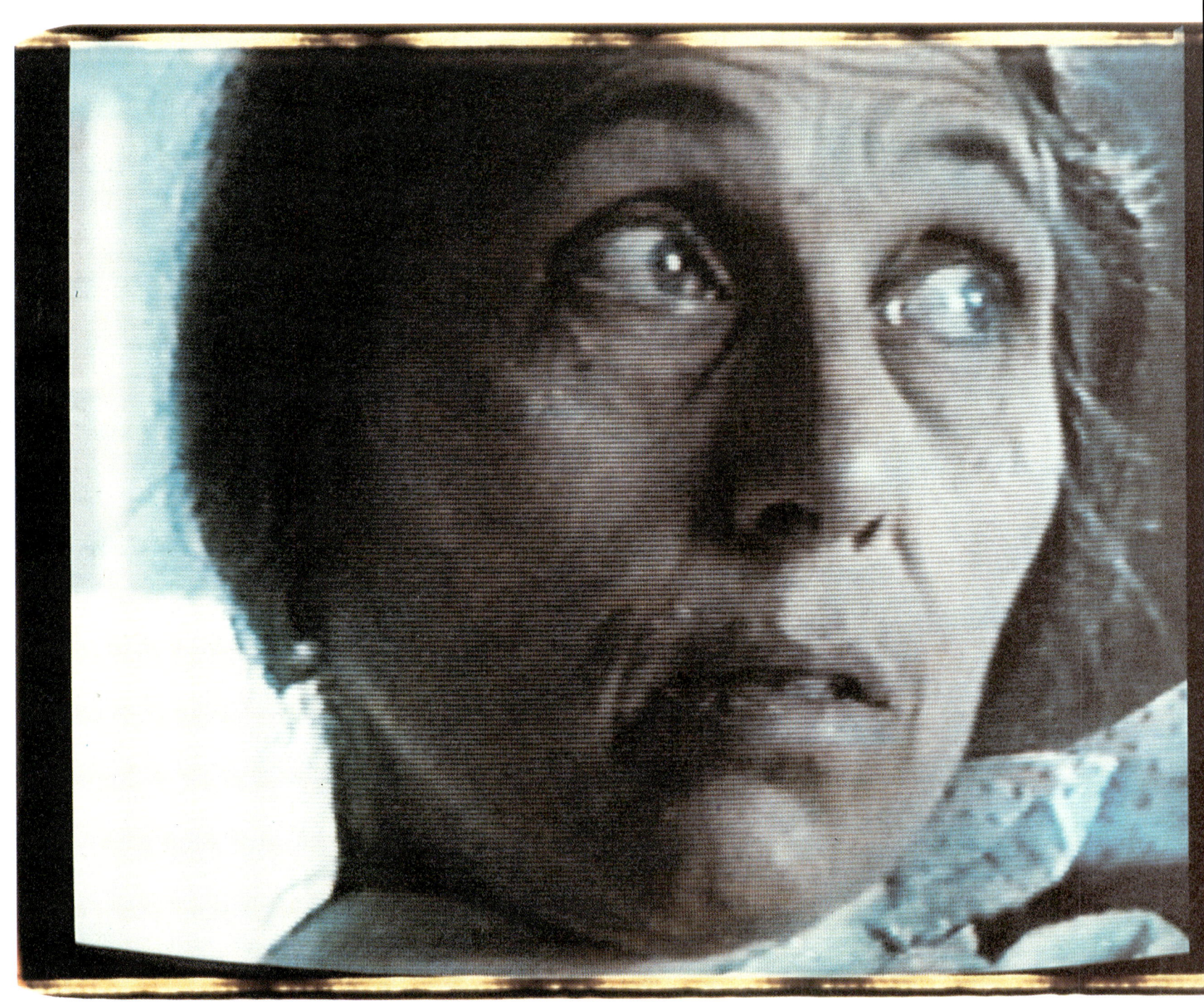

JUNE thinks and says: It's a love story...

PABLO says nothing…

Many have given me their help and their friendship
Werner Zryd – Sheila Curtis – Robert Delpire – Gary Hill
Anne Tucker – Kazuhiko Motomura – Reginald Rankin
Louis Faurer – Sid Kaplan – Rudi Wurlitzer
Peter MacGill – Vicent Todolí – Michal Hamner
Marty Greenbaum – Philip Brookman – Louis Silverstein
above all my wife June Leaf

NEW YORK / NOVA SCOTIA, January 1989